TO:

_____

FROM:

_____

HAPPINESS

IS A

WARM PUPPY

BY
CHARLES M. SCHULZ

PENGUIN WORKSHOP
An Imprint of Penguin Random House LLC, New York

© 1952 Peanuts Worldwide LLC. All rights reserved. This edition published in 2019 by Penguin Workshop,
an imprint of Penguin Random House LLC, New York. PENGUIN and PENGUIN WORKSHOP
are trademarks of Penguin Books Ltd, and the W colophon is a registered trademark of
Penguin Random House LLC. Manufactured in China.

Visit us online at www.penguinrandomhouse.com.

Library of Congress Cataloging-in-Publication Data is available upon request.

ISBN 9781524789954   10 9 8 7 6 5 4

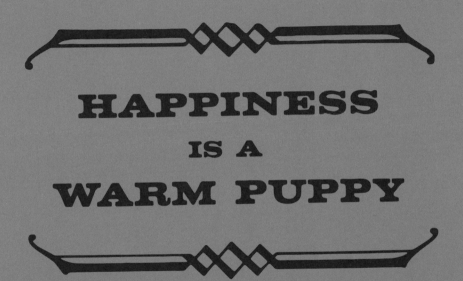

HAPPINESS
IS A
WARM PUPPY

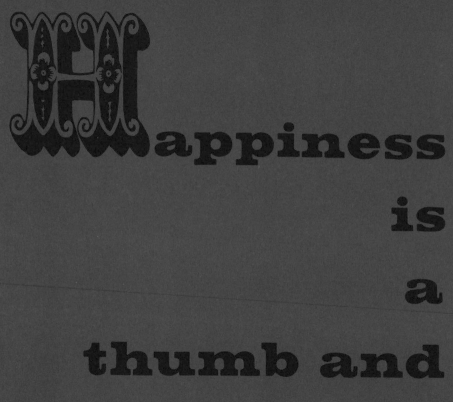

Happiness
is
a
thumb and
a blanket.

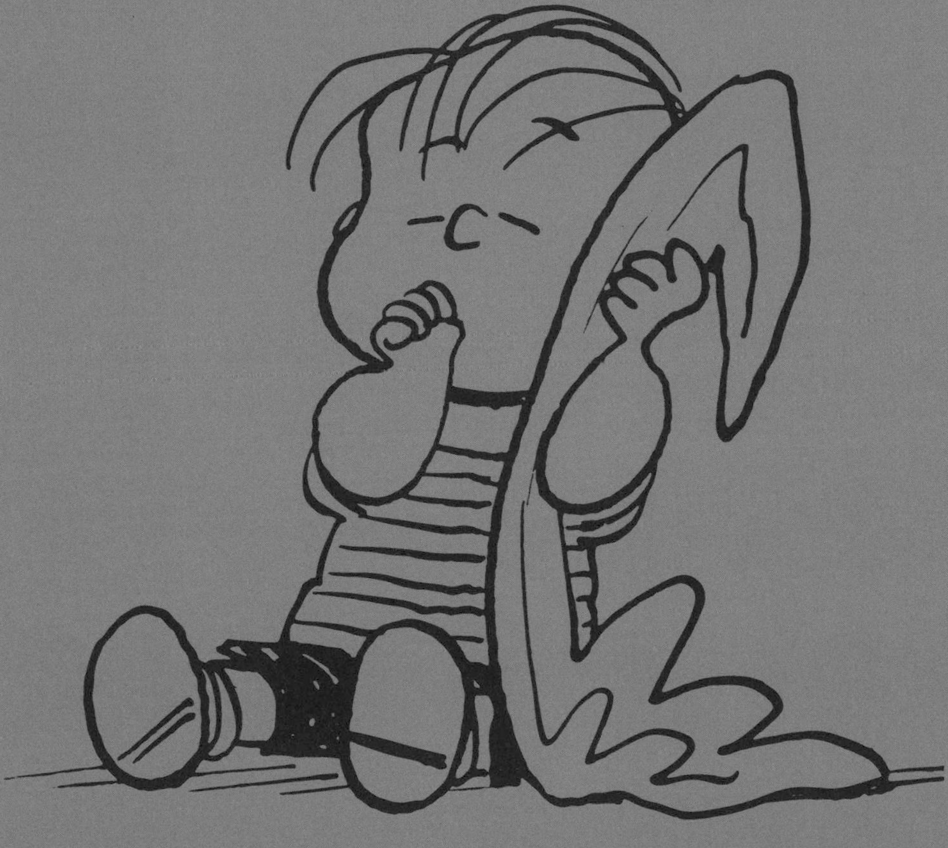

Happiness is an umbrella and a new raincoat.

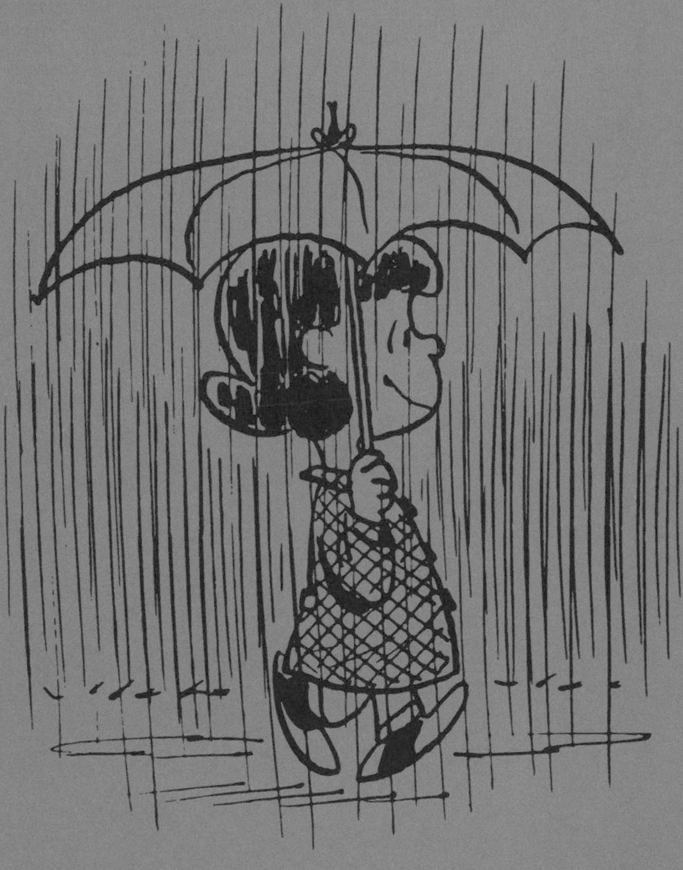

Happiness
is
a
pile
of leaves.

Happiness is a warm puppy.

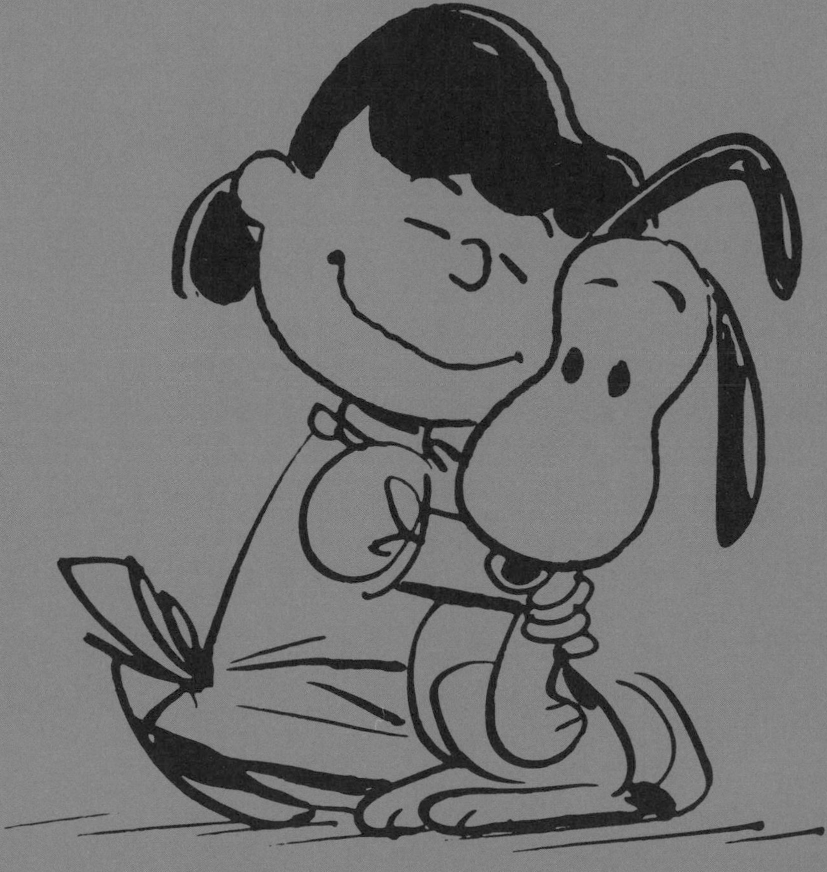

Happiness is an "A" on your spelling test.

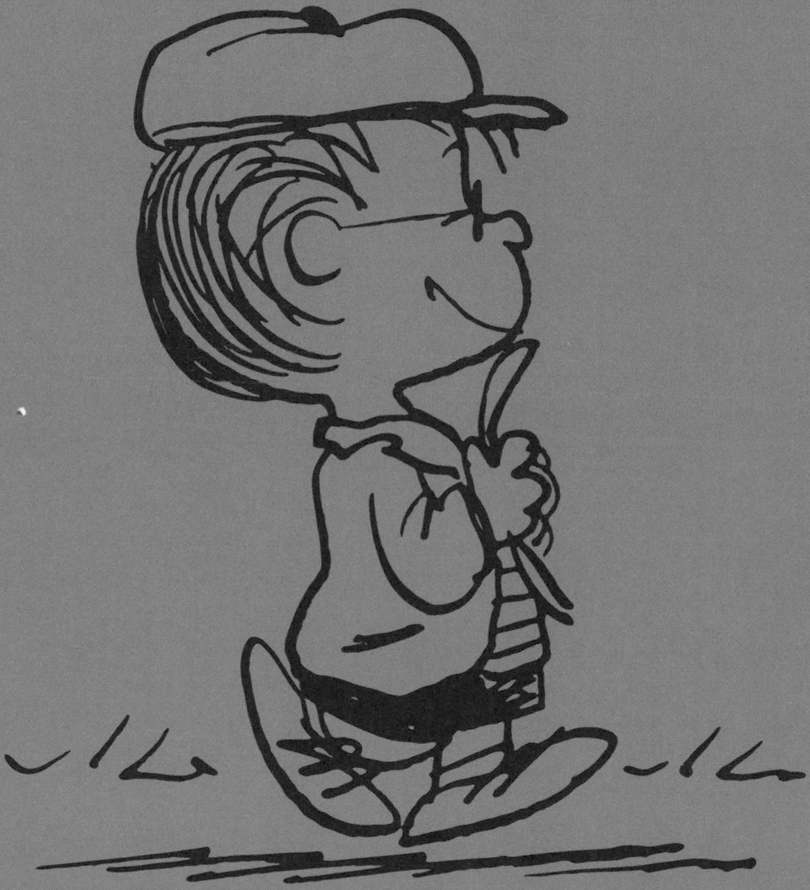

appiness
is
finding
someone
you like
at the
front door.

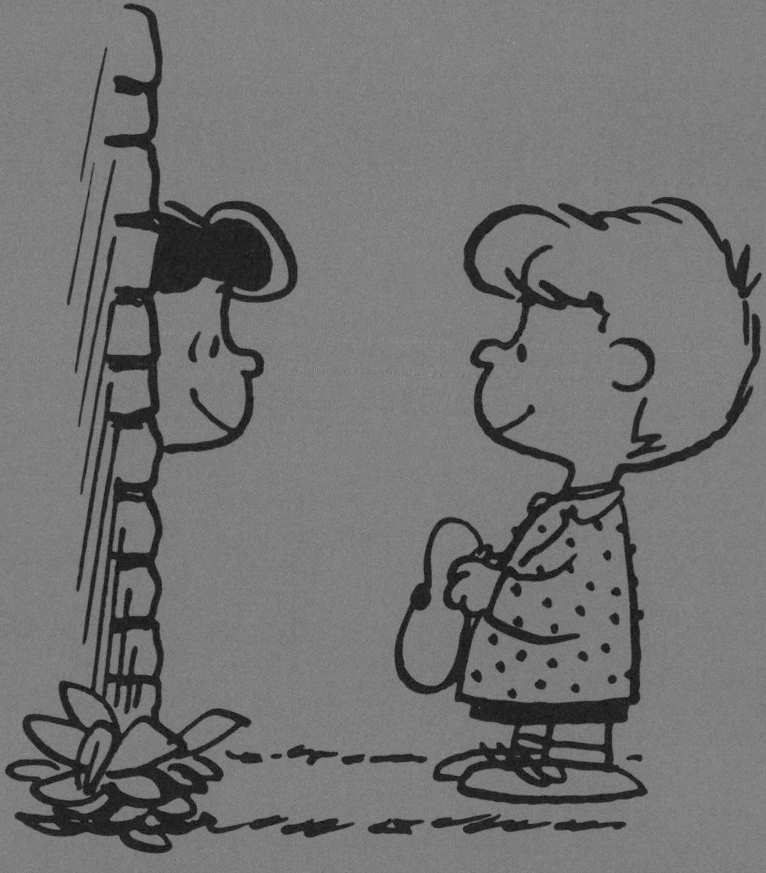

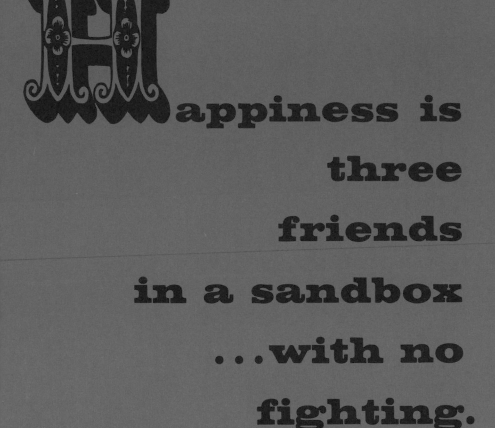

Happiness is three friends in a sandbox ...with no fighting.

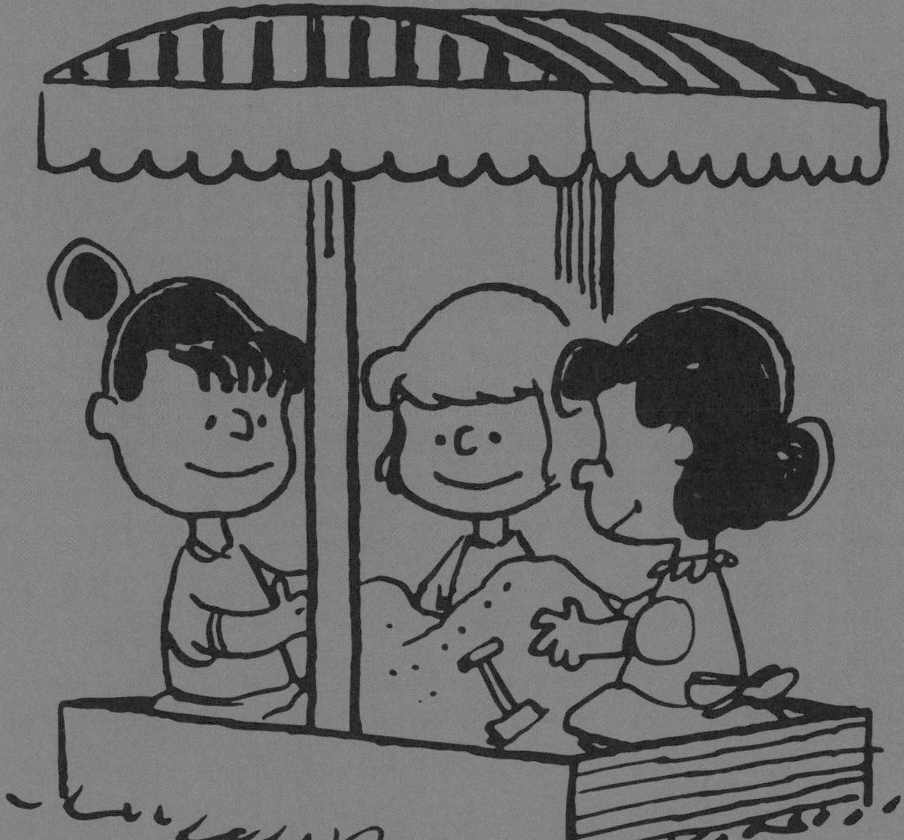

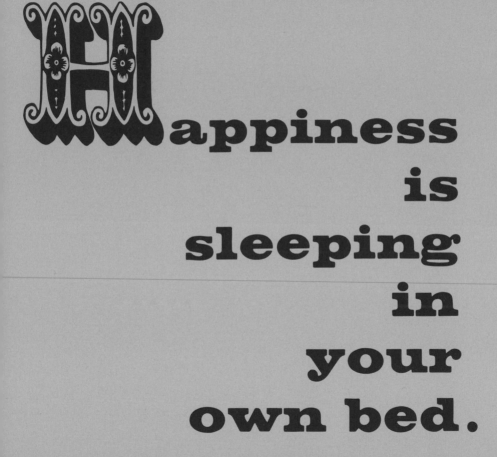

Happiness is sleeping in your own bed.

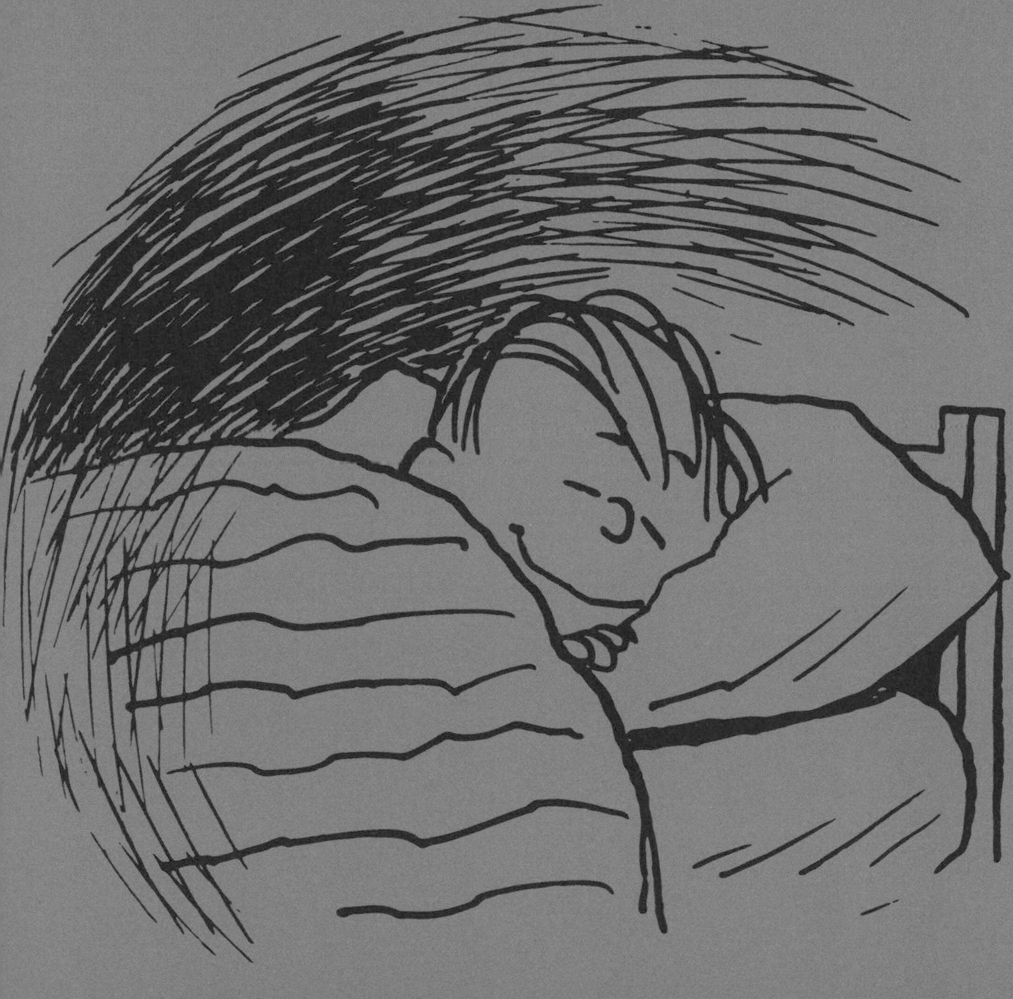

Happiness is a chain of paper clips.

Happiness is getting together with your friends.

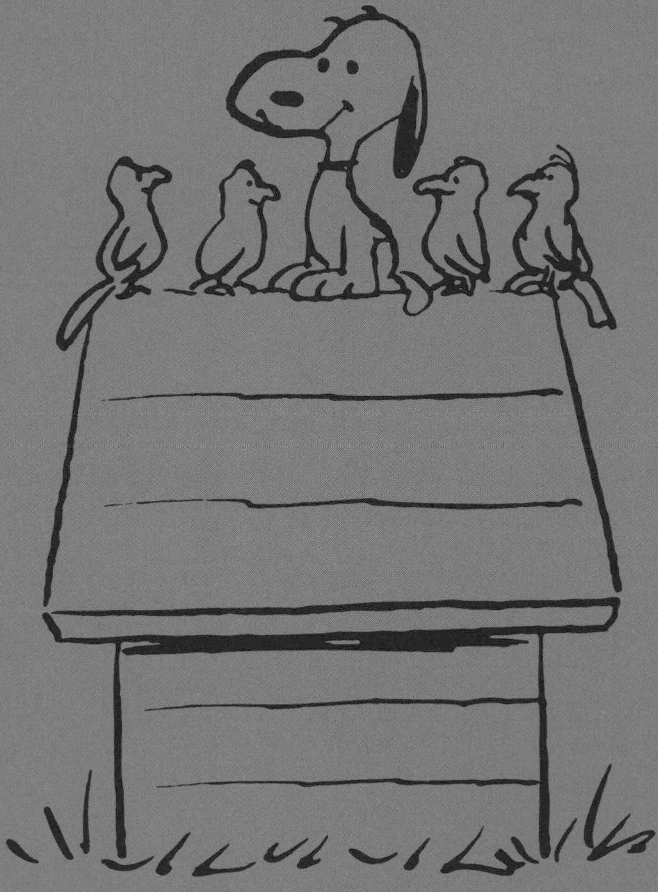

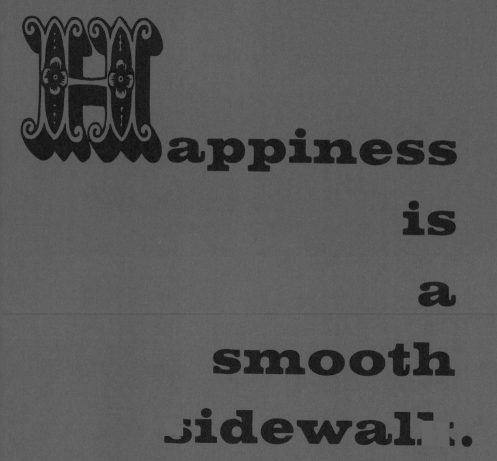

Happiness is a smooth sidewalk.

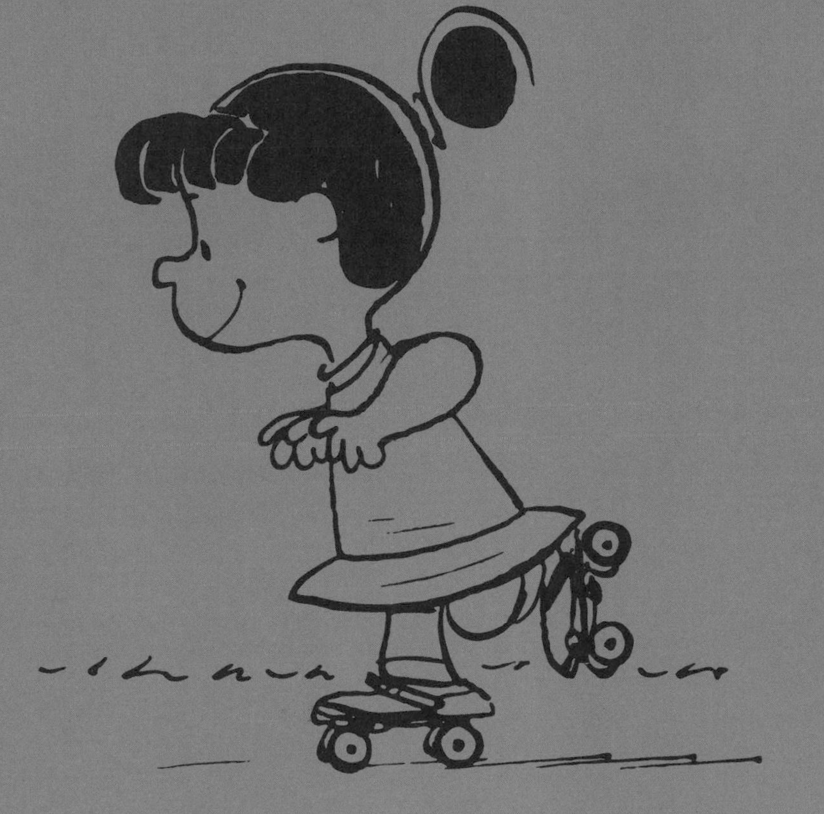

Happiness is finally getting the sliver out.

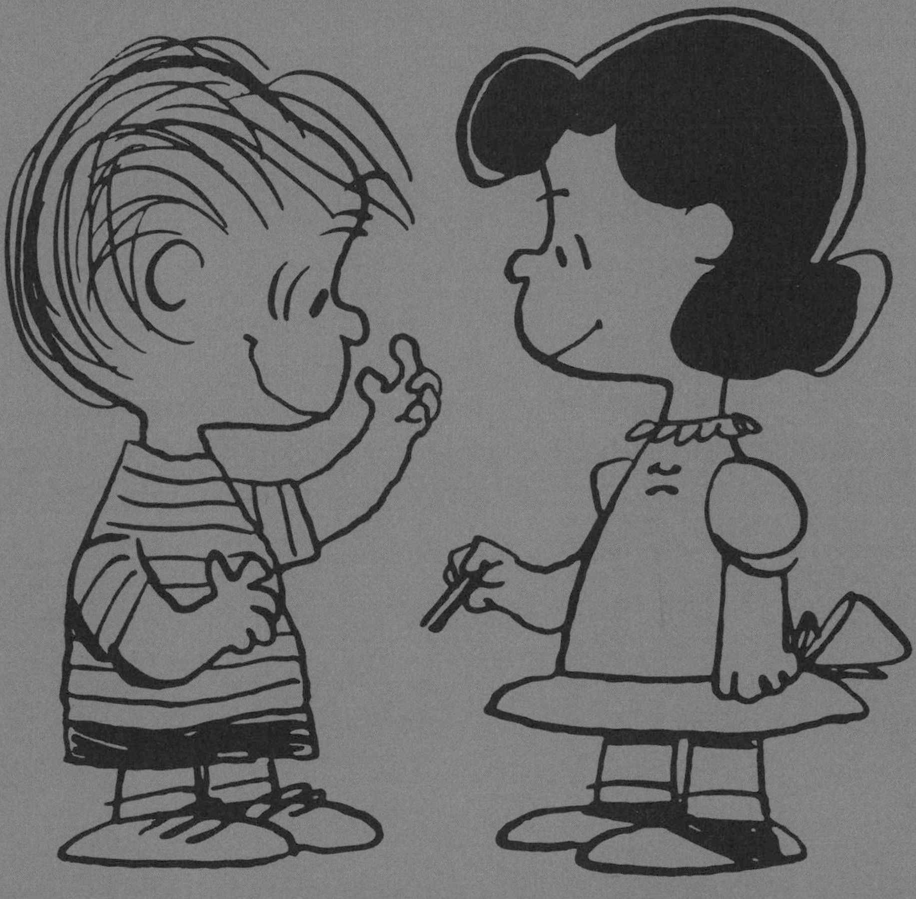

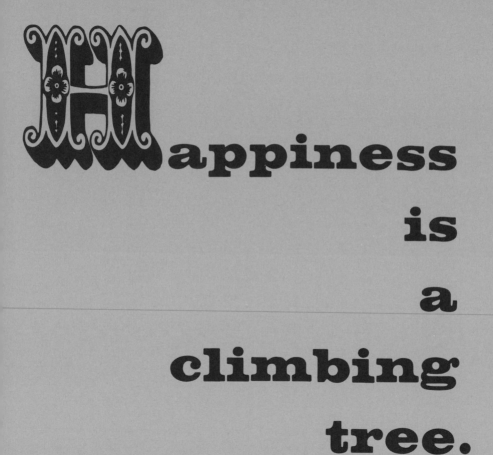

Happiness is a climbing tree.

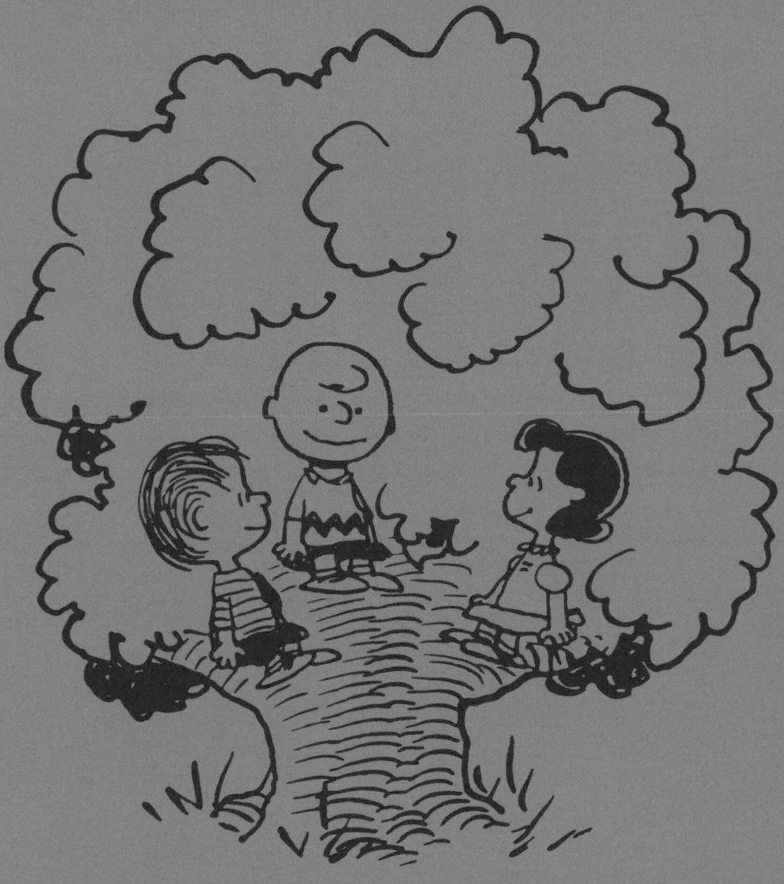

Happiness is lots of candles.

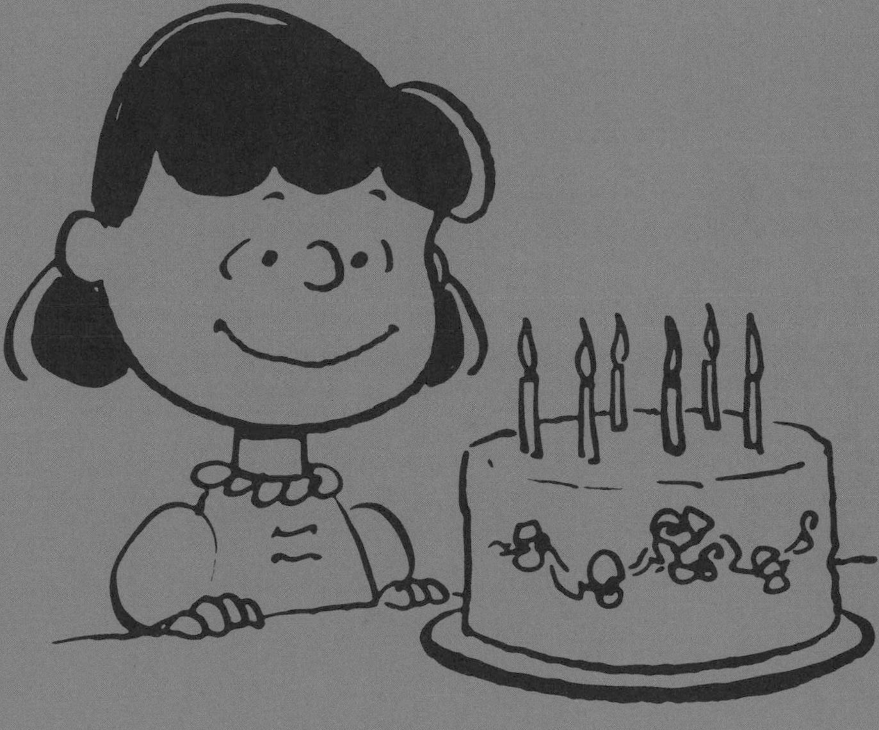

Happiness is being able to reach the doorknob.

Happiness is knowing all the answers.

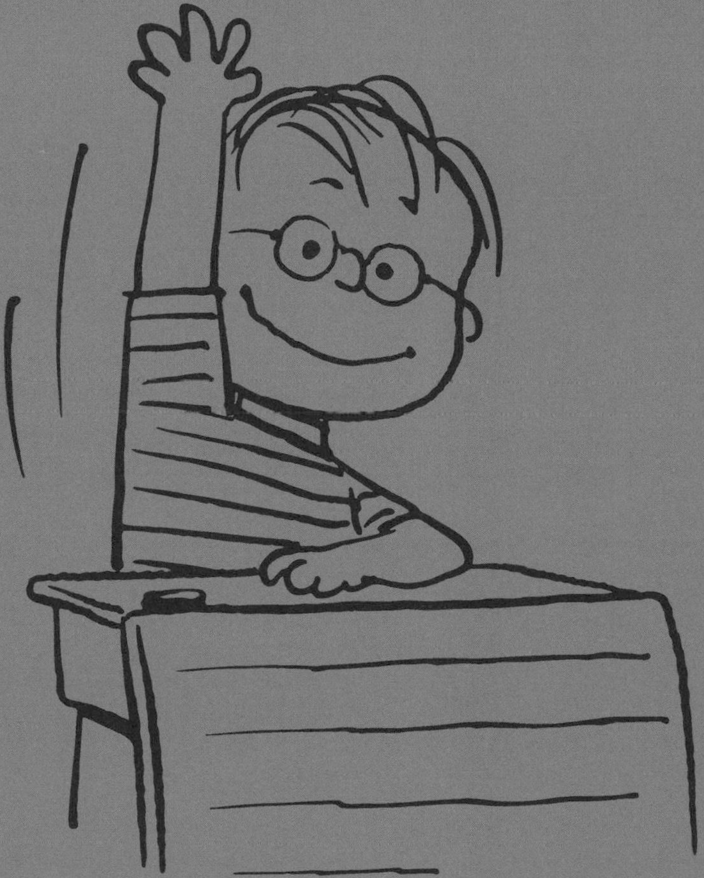

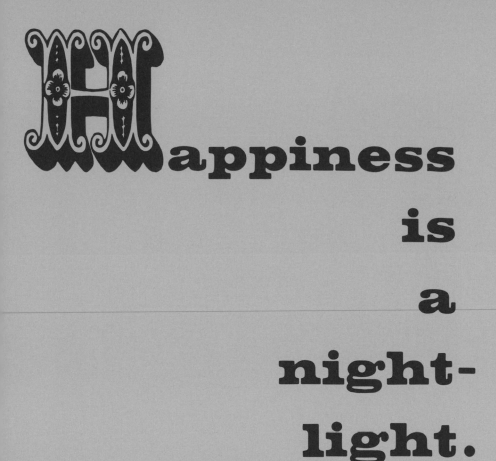

Happiness is a night-light.

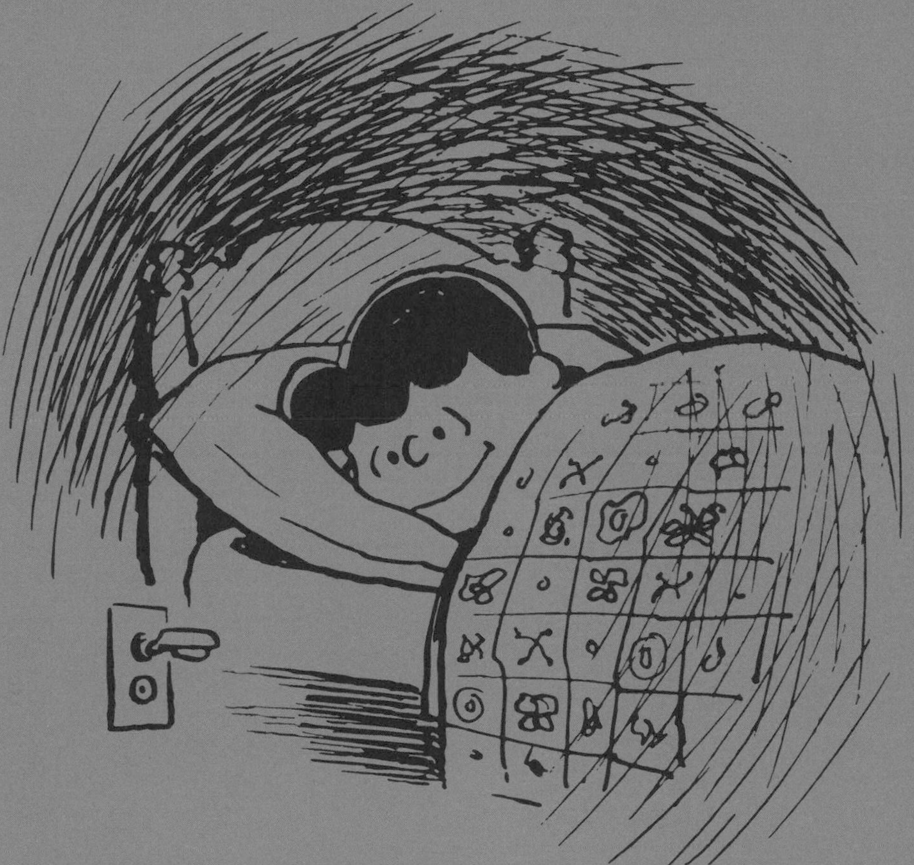

Happiness is some black, orange, yellow, white, and pink jelly beans, but no green ones.

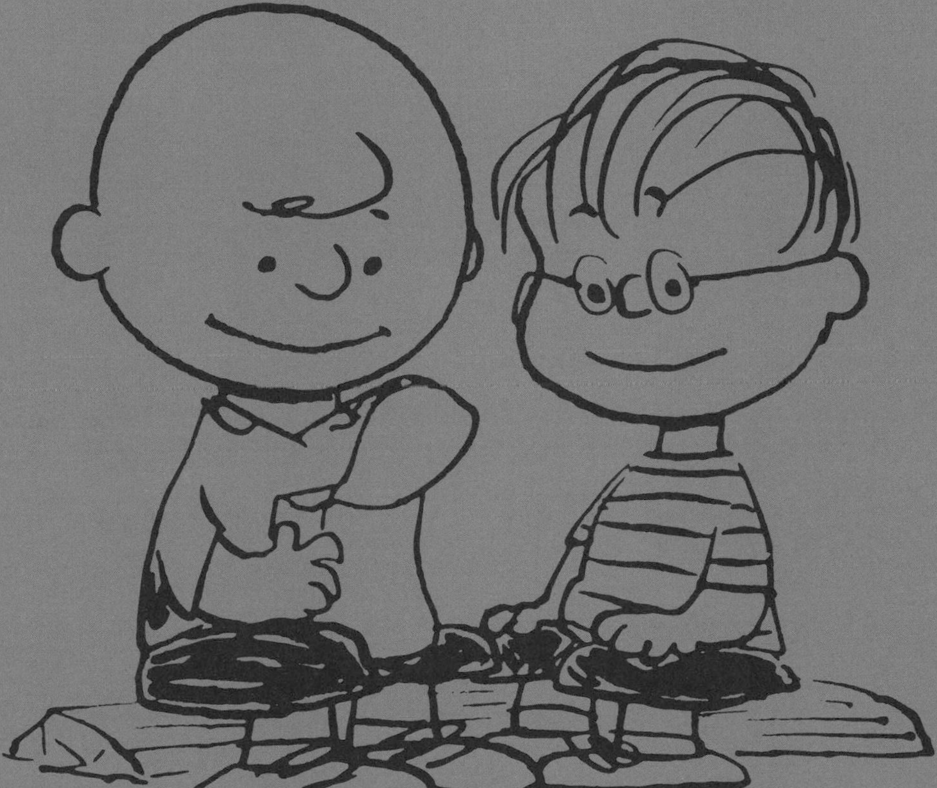

Happiness is the hiccups ...after they've gone away.

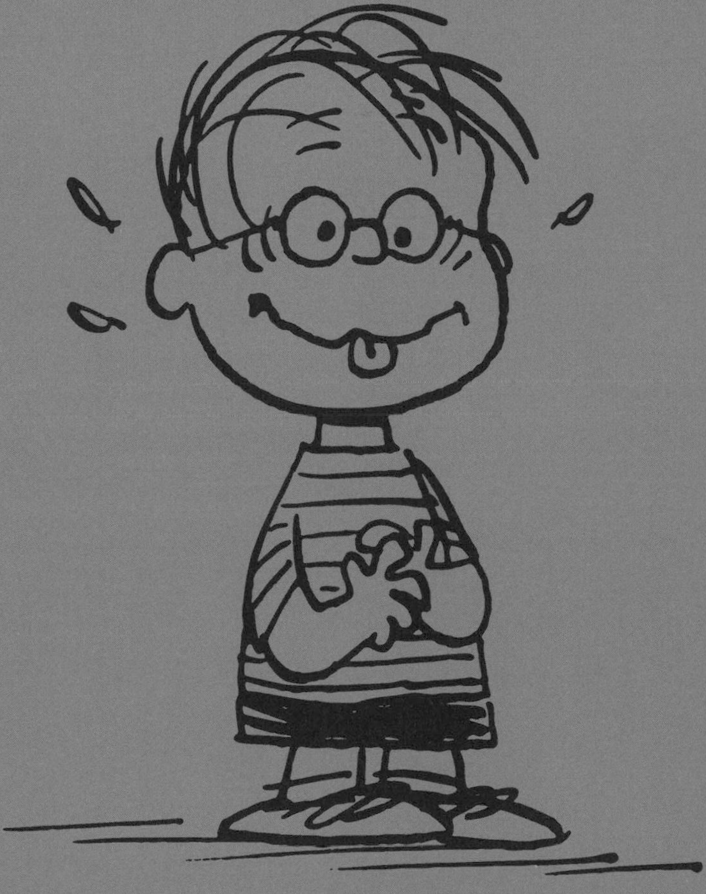

appiness is a good old-fashioned game of hide-and-seek.

Happiness is a fuzzy sweater.

Happiness is a bread-and-butter sandwich folded over.

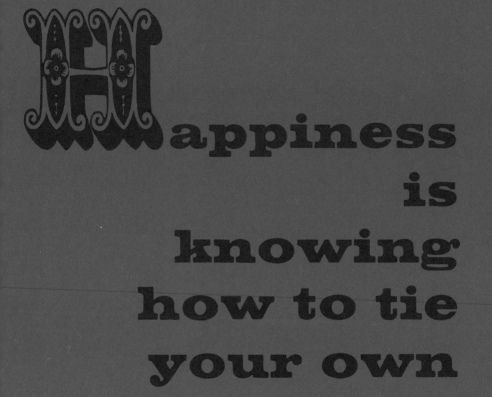

Happiness is knowing how to tie your own shoes.

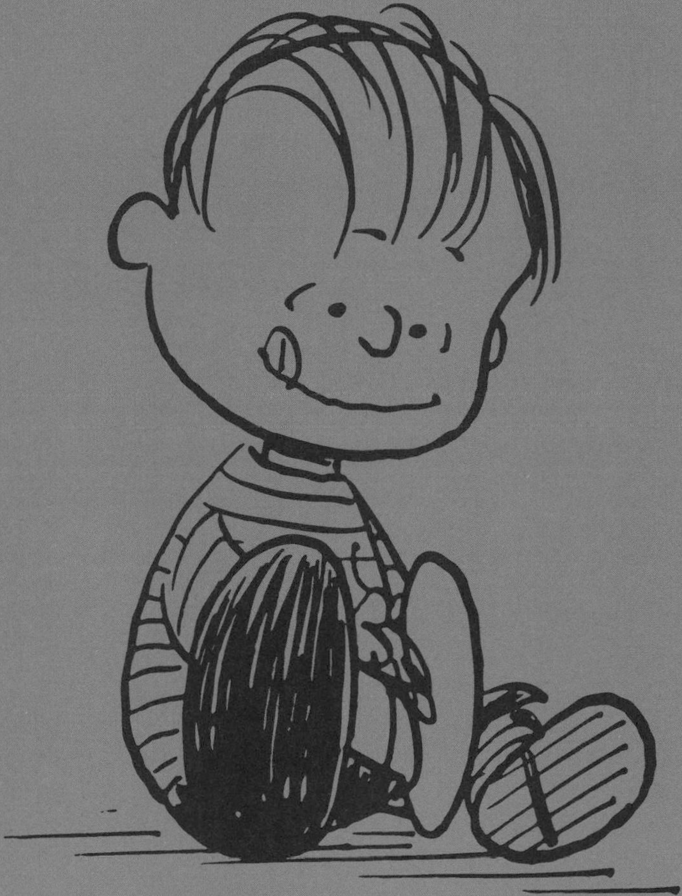

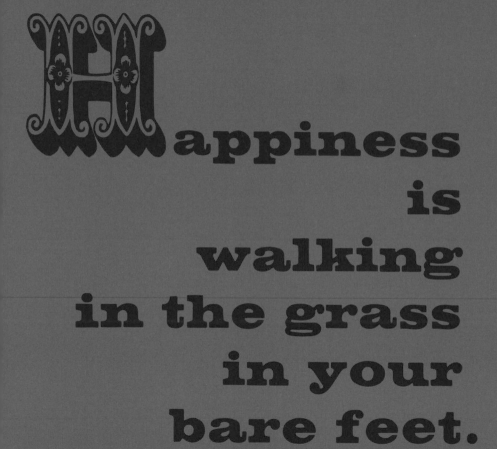

Happiness is walking in the grass in your bare feet.

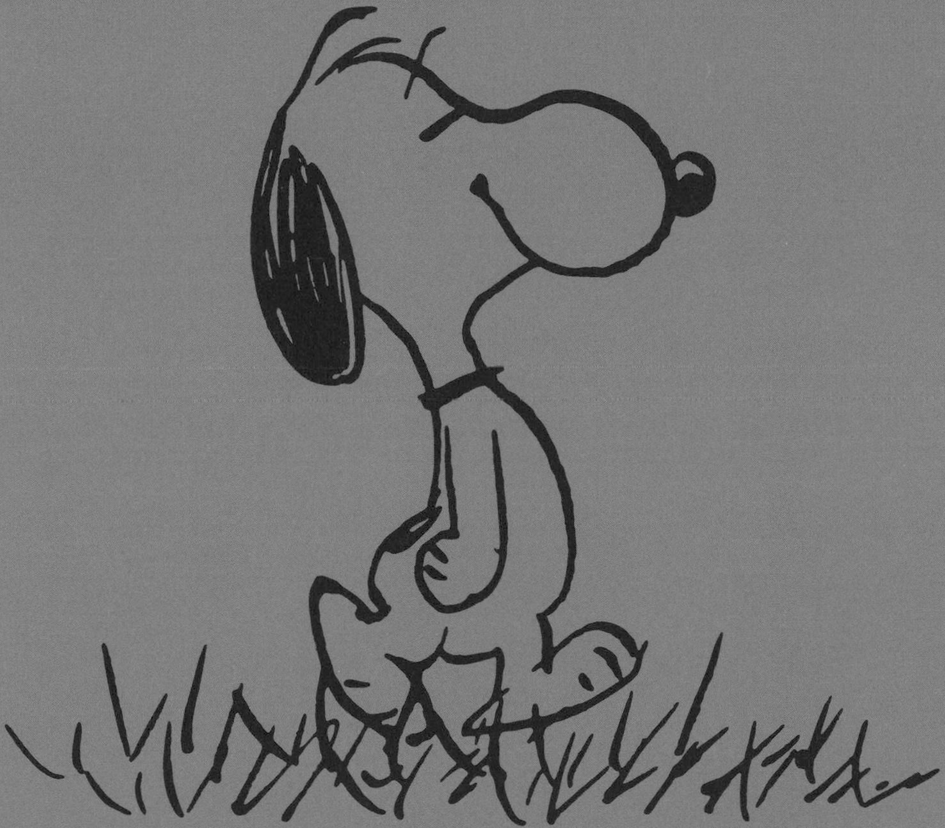

appiness
is
eighteen
different
colors.

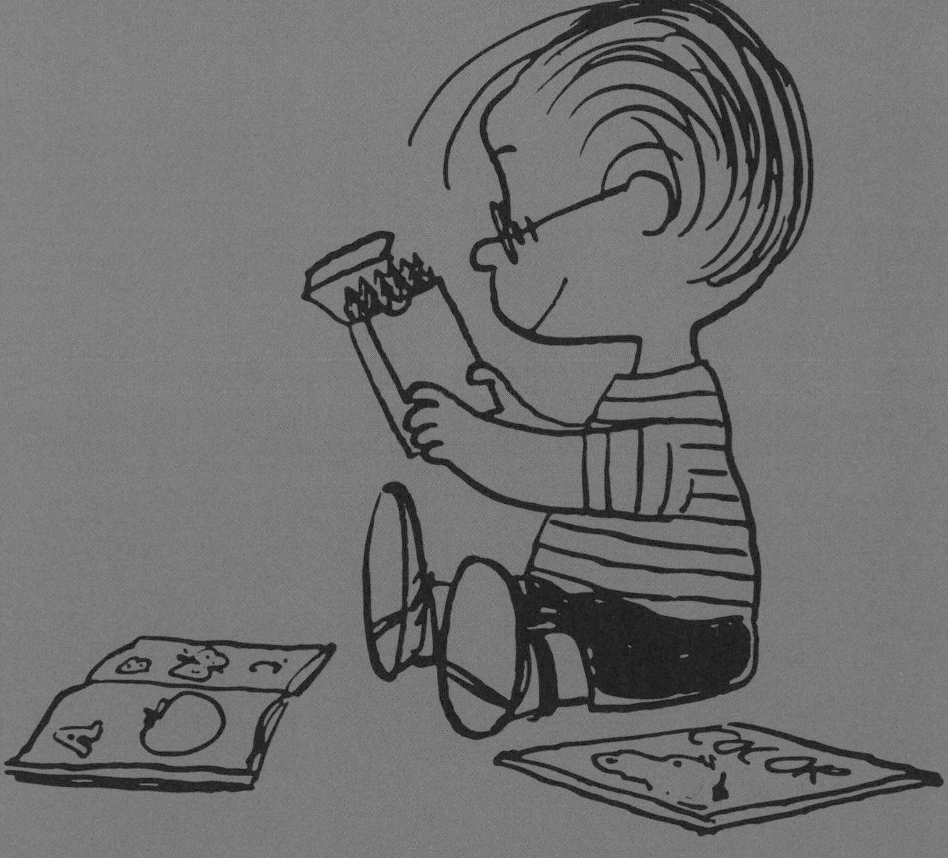

Happiness is a piece of fudge caught on the first bounce.

Happiness is finding the little piece with the pink edge and part of the sky and the top of the sailboat.

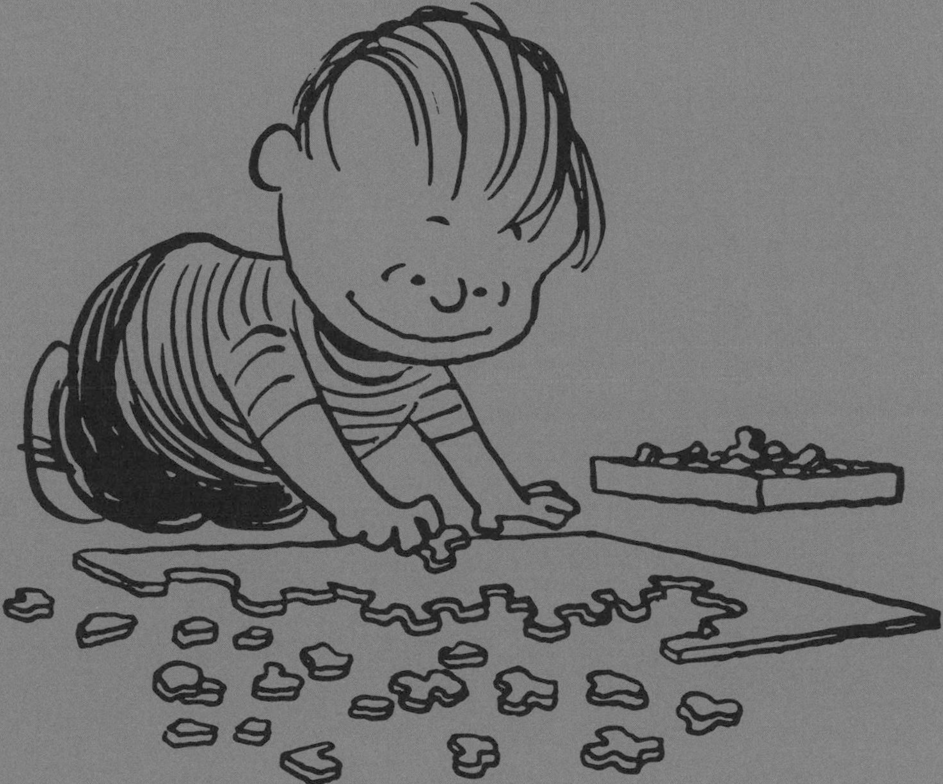

Happiness is finding out you're not so dumb after all.

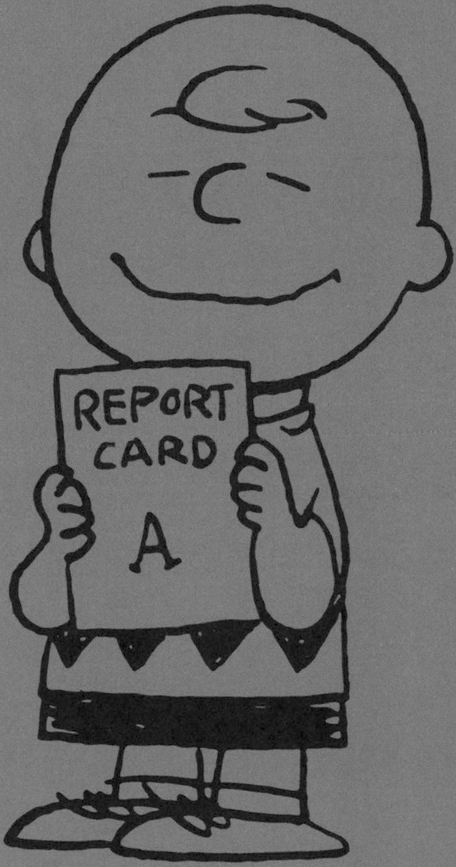
REPORT
CARD
A

Happiness is
t[redacted]irty-five cents
for the movie,
fifteen cents
for popcorn,
and a nickel
[redacted]o[redacted] a candy ba[redacted].

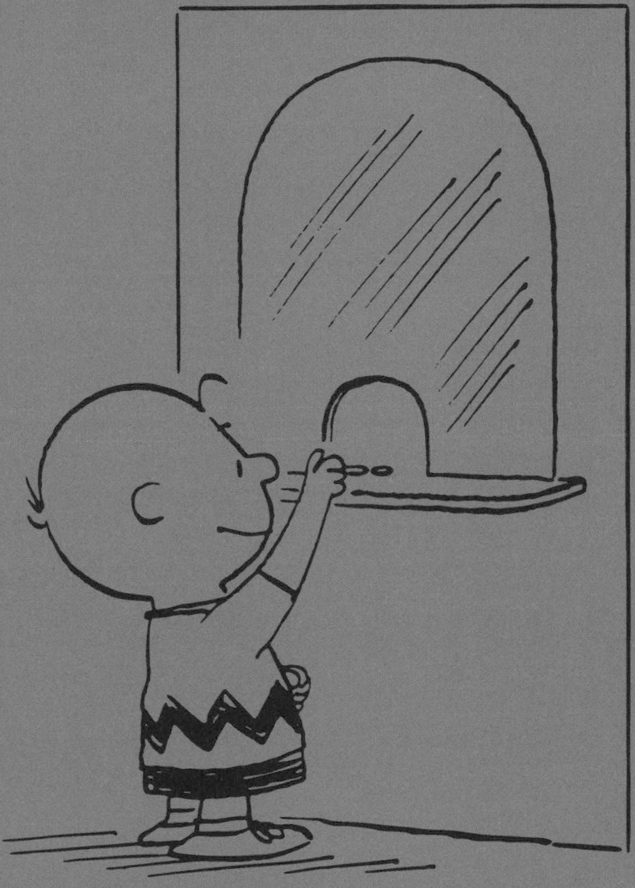

Happiness is one thing to one person and another thing to another person.

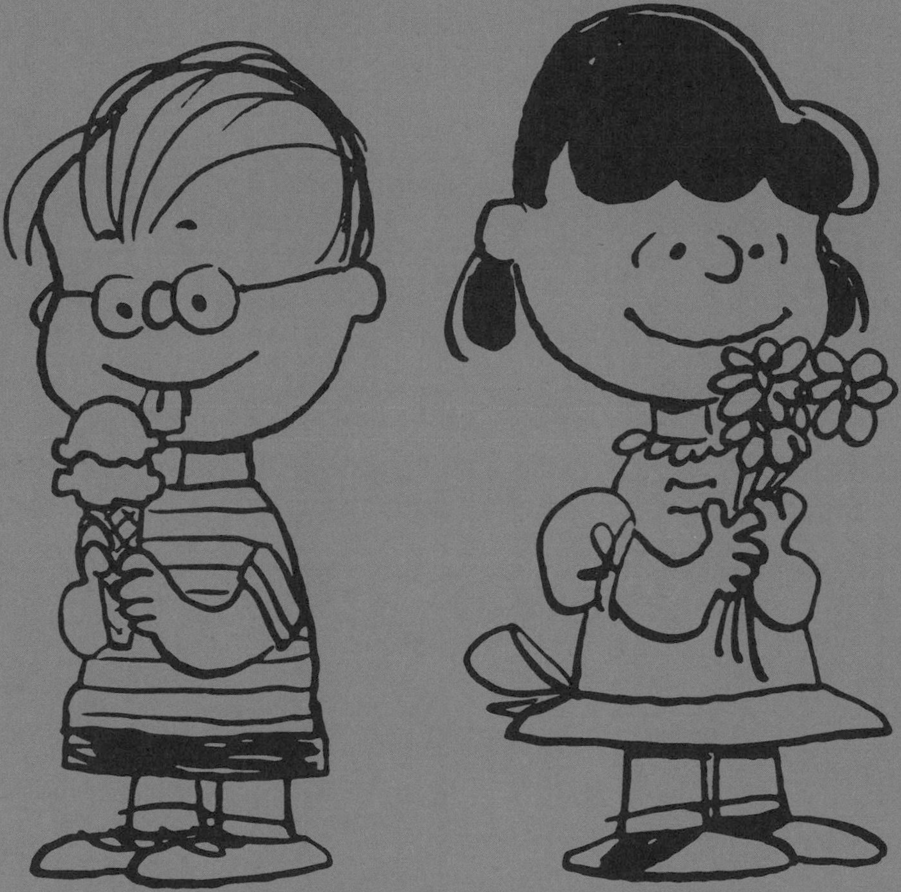